599.51   Althea.
ALTH   Whales

DATE DUE

DATE DUE			
DEC 1 8			
1-3			
24			
9/26			
MAY 1 0 1999			

WHALES

designed and written by Althea

illustrated by Barbara McGirr

Longman Group USA Inc.

Originally published in Great Britain in a slightly altered form by Longman Group UK Limited

ISBN: 0-88462-168-5   (library bound)
ISBN: 0-88462-169-3   (paperback)

Printed in the United States of America

88 89 90 10 9 8 7 6 5 4 3 2 1

Library of Congress Cataloging-in-Publication Data

Althea.
  Whales.

  (Save our wildlife)
  Summary: Describes the physical characteristics, behavior, and life cycle of whales.
  1. Whales--Juvenile literature. [1. Whales] I. McGirr, Barbara, ill. II. Title. III. Series: Althea. Save our wildlife.
QL737.C4A46 1988   599.5'1   88-8475
ISBN 0-88462-168-5
ISBN 0-88462-169-3 (pbk.)

Notes for parents and teachers
Save Our Wildlife books have been specially written and designed as a simple, yet informative, series of factual nature books for young children.

The illustrations are bright and clear, and children can "read" the pictures while the story is read to them.

The text has been specially set in large type to make it easy for children to follow along or even to read for themselves.

Whales live in water and swim,
but they are not fish.
Like dogs and cats they breathe air.
Dogs, cats and whales are mammals.
Fish are not.

Whales are of many kinds,
from small to elephant size.
These humpbacks are one kind.
They live in cold seas
during the summer months.

A whale can see under water
because it has oil glands
that stop the salty water
from stinging its eyes.

Every whale must come up
out of the water to get air.
It breathes in and out through
a hole in the top of its head.
Under water, a whale can hold
its breath for a long time.

Whales push themselves through the water with their powerful tails. Humpbacks use long flippers to steer and even to swim backward.

All humpbacks have different tail markings. Scientists photograph markings and use the pictures to learn where these whales go and if they always stay together.

Whales sometimes feed in groups.
Each whale eats as much as
a ton and a half of food in a day,
feeding mainly on small fish and
shrimp-like animals called krill.

In place of teeth, the humpback whale has rows of horny plates along its top jaw. They make a stiff fringe the whale uses like a sieve.

It gulps a great mouthful of krill and water. In goes the food, and when the whale closes its jaws, only water flows out. The stiff fringe traps the krill.

Humpbacks also eat herring and other small fish. A whale sometimes gets caught in a fishnet. Because it is so big, freeing a whale isn't easy.

Humpbacks use a clever way
to catch small fish they eat.

A whale circles below a
school of fish, sending up
a stream of bubbles.
The bubbles make a curtain
around the fish.

The frightened fish crowd
together in this bubble net.
Then the whale bursts up
through the middle and
takes a huge mouthful.

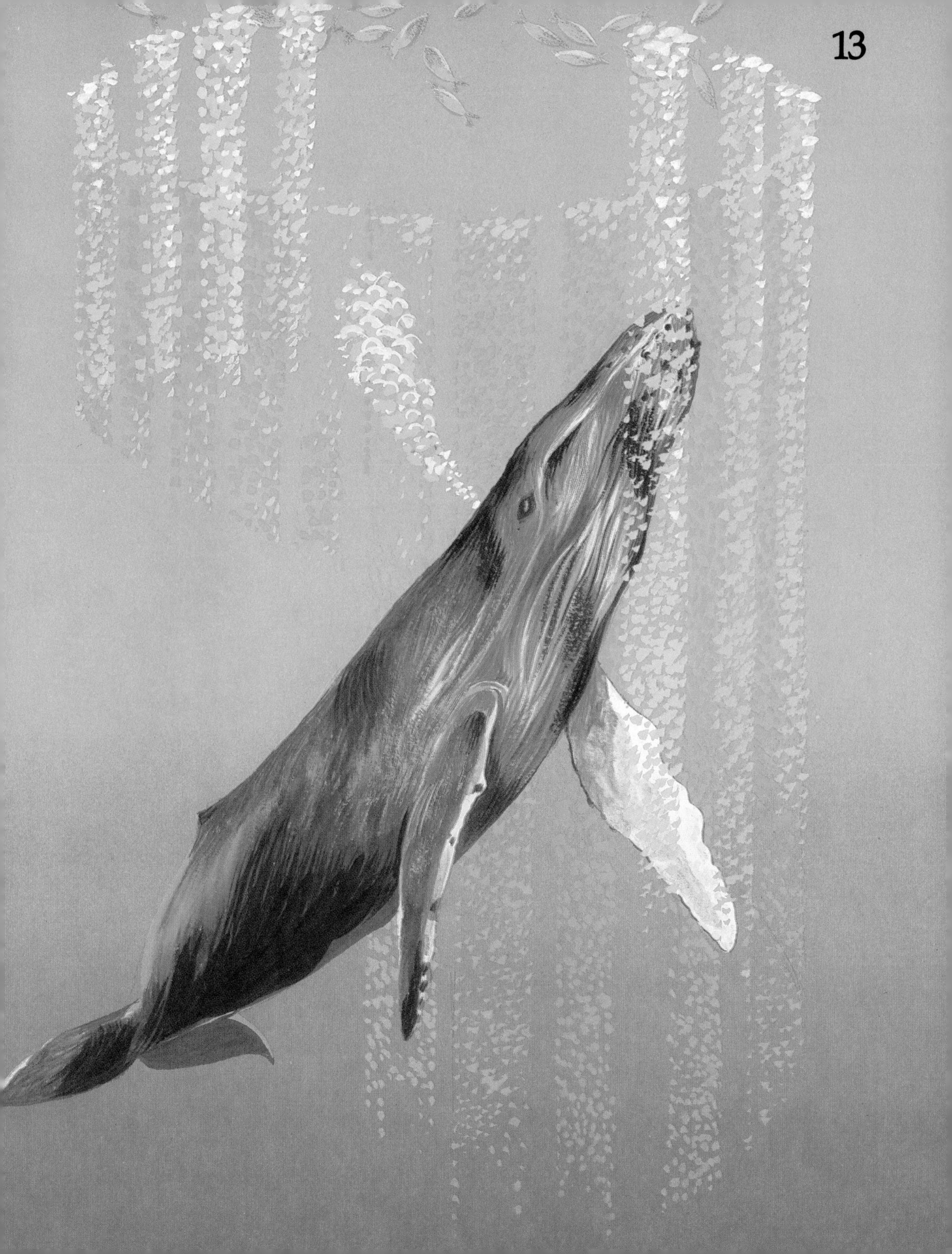

In summer months, humpbacks
live in cold seas near the Arctic
and Antarctic. Food is easy to get,
and the whales gain a lot of weight.
They build up thick layers of fat,
called blubber, under their skin.
This keeps them alive for the rest of
the year when food is hard to find.

By late summer, humpbacks in
groups migrate to warmer waters.
They swim slowly. The females
that mated the year before
and are pregnant lead the way.
Soon they will have their calves.

When a calf is born,
its mother pushes it to the
surface so it can breathe.
The calf then finds
one of its mother's nipples
and suckles her rich milk.

The young whale is fed
this way by its mother for
more than ten months.

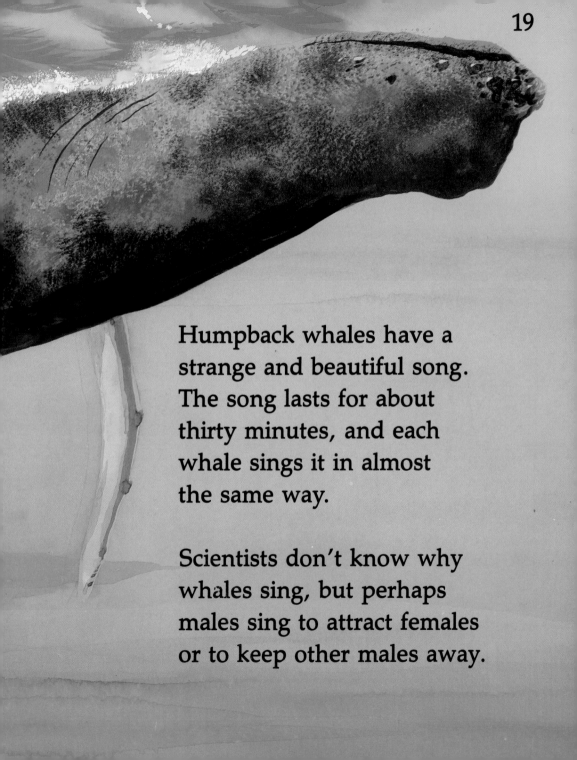

Humpback whales have a
strange and beautiful song.
The song lasts for about
thirty minutes, and each
whale sings it in almost
the same way.

Scientists don't know why
whales sing, but perhaps
males sing to attract females
or to keep other males away.

Humpbacks can leap right out
of the water, sometimes spinning
in the air and then smacking
the water with their flippers.
This may be play—or the males
showing off before the females.

When a male is attracted
by a female, he glides past,
stroking her with his flippers,
to persuade her to mate.

A female that mates
will not have her calf
until the following winter.
Usually a calf is born
every two years.

As the winter ends, groups of
humpbacks start the long journey
back to their summer feeding places.
The mothers with young calves
are last to leave the warm waters.

Humpback whales are not the largest of the whales, but they can reach a length of 50 feet. Their distinctive songs, available on recordings, have called attention to them, and although most whales use sound to communicate, the purpose is not clearly understood. These are, scientists agree, highly intelligent animals.

Whales are mammals. They have tufts of hair on their heads. They have lungs and rise to the surface of the water to breathe. The ability to hold their breath for long periods of time is vital to their feeding. They are warm-blooded, that is, they maintain a steady body temperature not dependent on their surroundings. When food is abundant, they build up heavy layers of body fat, blubber, to provide energy when food is scarce, as it may be during migrations.

The humpback belongs to the baleen whales, named for their mouth plates of baleen, or whalebone, through which small fish and plankton are screened. Whalebone is a horny material, like fingernails. A humpback and other closely related whales have distinctive grooves, sometimes called pleats, on their throats and chests.

For centuries, whales have been hunted by man for food, oil, and whalebone. Now as some whales are threatened with extinction, international agreements have been made to prevent overhunting. These agreements, however, are sometimes violated, and it is important to emphasize whales as endangered species.